What Oth

"Liam Corley's poetry collection *Unwound* accomplishes a rare feat of navigation: providing familiar territory for veterans, while leading citizens into uncharted waters. By calling to both sides of the civil-military divide, Corley's poems—clear, sharp, and evocative—remove bricks from that wall to build a bridge."

—Travis Klempan,
author of *Have Snakes, Need Birds* and *Hills Hide Mountains*

"As Liam Corley reminds us in his debut collection, *Unwound*, the work of poetry is to resist offering 'simple answers.' Instead, Corley takes us to places like Kabul and Farah, a modern landscape of acronyms, intelligence reports, medical forms, and the technical terminology of combat that nonetheless can't conceal how war leaves everyone wounded, the combatants and civilians, the perpetrators, victims, and bystanders. 'When that shit blows up,' Corley writes, 'people ask, What was that? / Oh, that's nothing, I say. / Nothing's happening.' But everything happens in these poems, most of all, the effort to unwound through lyric language, to unwind what can't be undone."

—Jehanne Dubrow, author of *Stateside* and *Dots & Dashes*

"Liam Corley's poems juxtapose the ancient and the modern, the beautiful and the terrifying. [...] The poems in this collection reveal the brutal absurdities of war and the consternation of returning to a divided nation in vivid, unsettling verse. Writing in the tradition of Elizabeth Bishop, James Fenimore Cooper, and Allen Ginsberg, Corley shows us— to paraphrase William Carlos Williams—it is difficult to get the news from poems, yet men and women die miserably every day for lack of what is found there."

—Jillian Danback-McGhan, author of *Midwatch*

❖ ❖ ❖

"Liam Corley's poems interweave specific episodes of war with general human experiences, and readers will find themselves alternately warmed and chilled by the results. Tension reports for duty in practical procedures, relationships, conversations, and a watermelon Jolly Rancher. Frustration stays in formation despite deploying with the army you have. Anger, mixed with despair, questions the choice to end '... worlds no bigger than a lover's spat ...' Throughout the book, Corley navigates an ambiguous undercurrent that makes us wonder what it means to represent the idea, the origin, the image, and the identity of America."

—Ben White, author of
Always Ready: Poems from a Life in the U.S. Coast Guard
and *The Recon Trilogy +1*

"Writing as a veteran U.S. Navy intelligence officer deployed to America's desert wars overseas, Liam Corley's poetic persona is a perfect fish-out-of-water, a thinking-man's-man ideally situated to stand watch between absence from family and the call to serve. Many poets explore what it means to experience war and return, but how many are brave enough to probe what it means to leave home in the first place? Truly a unique voice in 21st century war poetry!"

— Randy Brown, author of
Welcome to FOB Haiku: War Poems from Inside the Wire
and co-editor of *Why We Write: Craft Essays on Writing War*

Unwound

Poems from Enduring Wars

Liam Corley

Middle West Press LLC
Johnston, Iowa

Unwound: Poems from Enduring Wars
Copyright © 2023 by Liam Corley

All rights reserved. Except for brief quotations in critical articles or reviews, no part of this book may be reproduced without prior written permission from the author or publisher.

Poetry / Wars in Iraq & Afghanistan / Military Life

Unwound: Poems from Enduring Wars
by Liam Corley

ISBN (print): 978-1-953665-18-8
ISBN (e-book): 978-1-953665-19-5
Library of Congress Control Number: 2023937529

Middle West Press LLC
P.O. Box 1153
Johnston, Iowa 50131-9420
www.middlewestpress.com

Special thanks to James Burns of Colorado Springs, Colorado and Nathan Didier of Cedar Falls, Iowa!

Your patronage helps publish great military-themed writing!
www.aimingcircle.com

*To my wife, for holding fast
even when the night was long;*

*to my father, for showing me how to go to war
and then how to come back home;*

*and to my sisters and brothers in arms,
I give these words
as tribute and balm.*

CONTENTS

Small Wars & How They Start
unwound 3
Dogging the Hatch 5
The First Day 6
Small Wars Manual 11
Scout's Honor 13
Improvised Explosive Device 14
In-Country 16
Deerslayer on Furlough (Leatherstocking Poem No. 1) 17

Underway
No 'Ecstasy of Fumbling' 21
Suicide in Kabul 22
Spirits 23
The Other War 24
Foreign Policies 25
Care Package 27
CIVCAS Nine-Line 28
Transcript from the Night News 31
Something Else You Don't Need 32
Pathfinder and Chingachgook in Colloquy
   (Leatherstocking Poem No. 2) 34

Mentioned in Dispatches
BLUF (Bottom-Line Up-Front) 39
Intelligence Report 40
Negotiations 41
Heavy Guns at Alexander's Citadel 43
Uncleared 44
Carrying the Bags 45
Why the Cop Let Me Go 47
In Which I Serve as Outside Reader
   on General Petraeus's Dissertation 49
La Longue Carabine Grieves (Leatherstocking Poem No. 3) 50

Thank You for Sending Me
Dedication 55
Call Me Ahab 56
Thank You for Sending Me 57
One War 58
Reserves 59
Not Now that Strength 60
Dirt Navy 61
Recessional 62
Father Jacob Gets His Limp 63
Natty in the Stocks (Leatherstocking Poem No. 4) 64

Nothing / Happening
Terminal Leave 69
In Case of Emergency, Break This Poem 70
O.P.M. Hacker Blues 71
Double Rainbow at Dawn, 15 North at the 10 73
November 11 in Southern California 74
If You Give a Vet a Pencil 75
A Veteran Considers the Republic and Remembers Ginsberg 76
Leatherstocking in the Furnace (Leatherstocking Poem No. 5) 79
Frame of Reference 81
At the Children's Hospital 82
Hagar at Nine 83
Open Letter 84
The Task in Which We Walk Together 85

Notes & Acknowledgements 87
Glossary 89
A Few Words of Thanks 92
Author's Statement 94
About the Author 95
Also from Middle West Press 96

Small Wars
& How They Start

unwound

a poem for the other soldiers
citizens who never fired back

sleeping in armor
under a rifle's dead weight
crammed in rows

head drawn back in a helmet's grip
throat bare behind
a moistened Kevlar strap

for men sick in the passenger seat of a Humvee
head on a swivel for every fresh pile
ones for whom targets are never other
than black or white

do you sleep at night?
are you any better off?

I see you with a yellow ribbon wound
tight around your chest, looking down
when asked about the war

you who exercised your bolt with dry fires
unloading bullets on your rack
to let the spring of the clip unwind

inventorying them all:
sixty 9mm rounds,
one-hundred-twenty 5.56—no more than
90 seconds in a fight

LIAM CORLEY

taut in the night
until they are thumbed back
into the even pressure of
their orderly metal nest

smack the clip on a palm to settle the tips
and slide them all home

fifteen sleeping soldiers safe at your hip
thirty silent ones awake and heavy
around your neck

Dogging the Hatch

"Shave and a haircut—"

All those farewells
to make a clean seal: last
words, last kiss, last touch, last
meal.

The hatch between us now,
the gong of it slamming home,
spinning its locking wheel
like steering a ship
to port.

Is it you / or me
on the other side
where life is?

You / or me
whose held breath
consumes itself?

The cold sea rushes in, the all-
surrounding, unforgiving sea.

Here we have no control,
no sight of where we may emerge
from smoke and storm, only

the sere valves of our attention
tapping out
a semaphore of survivance:
                        "—two bitts."

LIAM CORLEY

The First Day

I.
When a man receives a letter demanding his presence
    for a specified term
of days pressing shod feet into another land's resisting earth,
    he considers
how his wife will best absorb the news that she will be as like a divorcée
with three kids as can be while still tangled in a love
that will grow surprisingly to resemble those first days
when long-desired but unexpected calls interrupted
dinner and made her shush the voices all around,
close the window, and hunker down.

Must he say, "I asked for this," or will knowledge that he swore
an oath to self and country suffice to adjust his covenant with her,
especially since swearing does not slacken love
but composes instead a remote dedication to her safety, shelter, and
    provision,
along with such benefits as accrue to kids who learn to walk
without him there to lift when they feel weak or step between
them and an autumn breeze that takes their breath in icy grip
and makes it short and hard?

Of the many ways to begin the drift from intimacy
to a psychic split made necessary when corporeal life sunders
and half the ingenious device proceeds under constant threat,
so much so that daily speech conveys no more than a litany
of mindless things, quotidian, banal, and yet still prized
because the blank passages of life are ones we most regret when lost,
being themselves patterns capable of sustaining
spendthrift gifts of time, attention, and regard,
should he elect the truth? Or begin

with formulas of regret that satisfy an unperceived but hovering cloud
    of witnesses
to this scene of first goodbye, a mob of later selves
who will look back on how the news broke
summer calm and made the weeks that passed before the one
in which he's ordered to report
compress themselves into a rolling ball that sheds home's moss
    and upsets
every other moving part?

LIAM CORLEY

II.
Opalescent in their opacity, the first words are,
"It's finally here," pronounced like a notice of eviction
a squatting tenant knew eventually would come after she stopped
paying rent and the owner saw the house going all to seed
without an ounce of benefit for the one who signed a contract
    in good faith
that the other party would deliver upon a given date a sum of money
or other valuables in kind equal to the cost of maintaining his estate
in the manner envisioned when he opened his mind to making terms
    with finite
creatures incapable of predicting whether their relationships or employ
would last until their lease was null and void.

Wordlessly, sheets pass from his hand to hers,
a premonition of other passings yet to come,
and he gazes at her widening eyes that fall in fits and spurts
    upon the page
but keep bouncing back to his because the military prose
    makes comprehension
flutter like a bird that's balked when it comes too near
    a wind-struck branch,
and eventually the man must use a finger to point
the date and destination summing
all she needs to know.

After that, speeches hang in throats, but kisses do not substitute
because her heart's already growing cold and his lips
taste like adultery or someone else's
wailing wall, recipient of tears and paper prayers
wedged into cracks where thousands of petitions went before,
    narrow graves
where slow disintegration admits space for yet another claim upon
the deity's unintelligible concern.

Phone calls gain the little facts that make no difference
beyond composing subject matter for a new kind of talk, a tic-tac-toe
of options, and yet a tithe of comfort comes in together fitting bricks
upon a path that no one else they know travels on today, a clever
muffling of the voice accusing them that loneliness is not
a new disaster, that other minds have found a way to master
empty evenings gracefully, or to at least defer
the breakdowns and destructive furies until after zero hour
when only walls and pillows will absorb the unrelenting blows
of daily tasks done differently because they're done alone.

Little ones emerge, but tightened eyes and shortened breath
    communicate
that something lacking innocence lurks in the shelter
once enclosed by parental limbs, and the sensitive child thinks
of nothing but to make a scene so she may put herself inside
the silent drama playing out within the house; mercifully
she's met by hugs and not the blasts that later come when her home-
less fears assault the fort where a mother isolates her heart.

LIAM CORLEY

III.
On that first night, they dine on remnants of former meals
since eating out seems false, public, and celebratory, and cooking would
    be petrol
on the fire of interrupted rituals once accepted as a normal life,
and the assortment of reheated dishes puts each person in a different
    world
of taste that replicates in gourmandic style how a table can comprise
infinities of space, as though the chow hall plates and MREs
the man will soon consume appeared as smoking apparitions
in the place he customarily assumes along the family board.

Some normalcy breaks in as daughters and a son brush teeth
and go sulkily to rooms they'll go to every night the man is gone
in the year to come, except for those they spend with relatives or friends
attempting to negate his loss
by providing stimulants for minds that mostly feel
    but only darkly can express
how the lack of him remains in a space above their heads
as they strive to fall asleep, looming like a cloud
between their eyes and stars
a hemisphere away, invisible because the sun
they watch depart and leave behind
a daily yet insipid gloom rises in the place where he
looks up and sees dying lights inside their room.

The first day ends in arms, a compact
unity of joint, mouth, and hip that strains between the separating souls
just as the curling fingers of a nursing babe stretch toward a face
above his edge of sight, the mother's flat, unfocused nose,
eyes, and teeth, not seen and yet believed to be as certain as the soft and
    sloppy jet of milk
between the infant's pursing, working lips and the sweaty
mess of cheek against the turgid breast, a miracle, a promise,
and an ache of weight.

Small Wars Manual
a parable

Say you heard about a marriage on the rocks—
awful husband, long-suffering wife. Say their unruly children
made neighbors nervous, screams and bottles
not contained to kitchen or yard. The house felt
even less secure when associates camped on couches or in corners,
man silent when they shot his wife full of smack.

Every room split into its own valley; their youngest tried
to live inside the walls. One daughter stretched an afghan
into a woolen fort behind a dresser.

At last, the neighbors decided enough was enough. Say a glass
    took flight
and shattered where other families walked barefoot.
They united, commissioned their best man, the finest husband
of them all. "Go in and make things straight," they say.
"Show that wreck how to raise a family right."

So in he went, all fists and a bottle of wine. Things calmed
down quick. "Here, now," he said as he poured
the wife a glass, table set with take-out Italian, "Tell me
about your day," leaned back and let her litany
swallow night, left-hand twisted in the collar
of the snarling husband's shirt.

Associates moved out double-time, the ones that didn't squeeze
into cracks vacated by children exiting the walls. Spankings
grew infrequent, even if a few arms were still smuggled in.
When the errant spouse caught his wife by the hair, the finest one
broke his wrist. "You must learn," he said, "how this is done,"

LIAM CORLEY

and smoothly had the woman shower before he brought her pleasure

in their bloodstained bed. "This is how you kiss
and make up," he said, dipping the woman toward
    a pool of cash. The best
man smelled of cologne and working appliances. The children
liked new clothes and bicycles not yet hocked for another fix but
weren't impressed by directives to respect a lunatic
who claimed them as his own.

"Now then," the deployed man said after a night
    when both eyes were bruised
as he slept between the happy couple, "I've shown you how
to take life's ups and downs. You can be a happy family if you'll only
just decide." Leaving behind several dry-cleaned suits, the best man
pulls out at dawn. Say his own kids had forgotten how great
he was. Say the finest husband's wife didn't like the clap
he carried home after fucking someone else years on end.
Say this was all a butterfly's dream and
every happy family is happy in their own way.

Scout's Honor

The struck dog on the side of the road
is waiting for the driver to come back
and inquire. Old ladies pile up
next to him, queuing for their chance
to cross. A wrapper blows into the gutter,
adding to the confusion. Meanwhile, a neighbor can be heard
calling from a roof where the ladder has been lost;
the antenna he adjusts still hasn't found
its best reception. Soon children will be dismissed
from school, mouths slavering
for the chocolate bars some passerby
will doubtless offer them from the back
of a van, and a teenage driver will speed past
using her probationary license.

Though you try hard, you can't remember why
you rescued the paper from the morning sprinkler,
carefully spreading its pages to dry. When you peel
the world off your kitchen table, sodden protesters
leave their faces behind, ragged specks that tear
the eyes widening in the polished wooden grain.

LIAM CORLEY

Improvised Explosive Device

> *"[Y]ou go to war with the army you have."*
> *—Donald Rumsfeld, U.S. Secretary of Defense*
> *1975-1977; 2001-2006*

The serpent line winding through the plank-floored
warehouse of the marsh-aired Fort Jackson distribution center
got me so pissed that I smacked my fist
into ceramic plate and hissed sotto voce,
"There's got to be a better fucking way."
Civilians every few yards supervised bins
overflowing with stained armor parts: chest plate, back
plate, groin shield, side panel, shoulder wrap, knee and elbow pads
in small, medium, large, extra-large, and a barely molded
female version to cause a little less pain in the breast.
Our parts came from at least a dozen soldiers
whose armor had returned from deployments before ours.
On this black-flagged South Carolina day, glistening drills barked,
"Hydrate,"
throughout the battle rattle hour we spent
fumbling with MOLLE straps and half-exhausted
Velcro fittings on Kevlar compartments. Now I understood
the bake sales for Dragon Skin Armor requested by buddies
who claimed that Army IBA failed after only one shot.

In Kabul, every broken piece of gear we kept
in makeshift service was marked TAYH, the army you have.
The Taliban mastered making do with scrap
we'd given the mujahideen and materiel Iran began to smuggle in.
When dismembered Humvees lolling off a smoking curb hit primetime,
Seabee welders busted out some heavy plate and a Pentagon
logistics guy coined a magic phrase because it mostly worked:

UNWOUND

"up-armored" trucks were all the rage no matter what the prefix said
about the canvas doors we had at first.

I sit now with a writer who is blocked, and I think
Rumsfeld could have been our secretary of poetic
state. The Taliban are still kicking ass; even their ghazals
explode. Take up your pack, friend. All our MFAs
went to Iraq, and the rotator for Kandahar leaves tonight. Go to war
with the words you have. Magazines will come after.

LIAM CORLEY

In-Country

The dog-tag laced to the right boot
winks an S-O-S from its unmarred
metal face whenever the
yellow sun
tungsten lamp or
Surefire personal illumination device
reflects to interested eyes
the bearer's
religion
blood
parental application of a name, and place
in the inventory of the state.

The other boot is left
with no sign it will ever drop,
its severe mate testimony
to the old saw that right
sometimes gets lost
sometimes gets in the way
of coming back in one
piece.

The necklace tag reflects little
other than the promised
repatriation of remains,
a covenant against stately graves
established in preceding wars
and set in places citizens would like to visit.

No such guarantee insures returning heads
or their cargoes of haunted valleys
electric firings and bruising
pulses of subterranean light.

Deerslayer on Furlough
(Leatherstocking Poem No. 1)

The Leatherstocking Tales (1823-1841) are a series of novels by James Fenimore Cooper, the best-known of which today may be The Last of the Mohicans. The 5-book series tells the story of one of the most beloved characters in American fiction, Nathaniel "Natty" Bumppo, a white frontiersman raised and educated in Native American societies. He is called by many names, including "The Leatherstocking," "Hawkeye," and "La Longue Carabine."

This poem follows Bumppo after he has been captured by Iroquois warriors and furloughed for one night as a sign of respect to his honor.

I won't deny my pride is touched more than my fear,
though I think a body who gives himself airs
is like a frog listening to the lake give back
his voice in thunder. Doing right has a cost, that's certain,
like when a hunter wounds a beast and must give himself
to chase, no matter the thorny copse or winter squall
it flees through, else the buck would die to no purpose.

If a man would kill, it should be for some higher end, and I hold
the same is true when that man should die. No great virtue
comes from waste. My gifts are man's gifts, certain,
and no tears should spring from me keeping my word.
I want to live, but only a living that's pure and right and strong.
I'd have no rest knowing I'd done wrong and would find no honor
    passing days
I couldn't look on a calm forest pond and see my own clear eye.

I am stubborn, lass; I own it. Few things enough are truly ours
that we can bring them with us when we're gone: choices

LIAM CORLEY

we can be proud of, faces of them by whom we've done right, the quiet,
grateful chorus sung by the heart in a starlit, restful night. Oh, I know
you can't see this as I do. No other man's duty looks as certain
as our own. But what I ask you won't deny: honest words,
open ears, undimmed eyes, a night
and a morning before I'm gone.

I'll make a fire. The warriors in the woods
will wait. This burning cooks my meat tonight
and warms my friends; tomorrow's flames
will lick my bones.

Underway

No 'Ecstasy of Fumbling'

Delivered in moments the eyes, mouth, and small
muscles of the gut are completely relaxed,
a broadcast of shards sears into an endless
night news. These are the times tried men fail
to reason or, more commonly, freak out, while others
are sucked instantaneously into chambers
wholly evacuated of sense. Bound to decorous
uses of language, reporters squeeze furrows
on youthful brows and fall back on questions
of ballistics, asking witnesses what they felt
when the bomb went off, what they thought
it really was. A sucker punch of air
the most observant would say before her skin
puckered in slow incineration, her brain
entertaining thoughts that once escaped a soldier
two heart-stopping legs from war
when the unbelievable toss out of left field
interrupts his final approach and he is tagged
out—no missed signal or hunch to slide:
the game just ends.

Stands empty as he rests
in the field, limbs stiff from the unbroken acid of strain,
eyes fixed on batteries that wink out in stages,
inadmissible proof that terror is nothing
the organs can filter alone, a message he's not able
to retrieve. Leaving viewers to meet God in their own time
and place, impatient announcers cut this story short,
producing a gap in the language between Y
and Z, the point of the iceberg
I'm under.

LIAM CORLEY

Suicide in Kabul
reported while under Gen. Stanley A. McChrystal's command

I see a body bleeding
from the skull and say
"Must be an exercise"
despite the sweaty
grunting stretcher crew
humping fast and
silent on my right
with a fleshy jiggling boy
whose faceless face and dangling outstretched arms
splay so unaffectedly
I think he's acting.

When we later learn of all
that made him kill
himself, we scoff at worlds
no bigger than a lover's spat
and general discontent
so easily
blown off.

Before we box
the boy's effects
for his Next of Kin,
Chaps puts them
in required forms
and briefs him
up the chain.

Spirits

I have fought
hotel balcony demons.
I have looked
away from open bays and prayed my feet
to flooring wedged between steel girders
as drafts tore through the suite and out.

Shipmates, hear me now:
draw curtains on the chittering prinks
and do not think
how much you'd miss your spouse, son, daughter,
life if you tumbled through the unlocked sash.

Let's be clear: you've got yourself
a demon. Your voice is not
the susurrous score.

Torpid as glutton crows, devils bloom
on acid shed by lemon souls like ours. As horn flies cluster
on a wound, so too they bark their claws
on soaring walls and wait
for the opening jar of undecanted tomb.

LIAM CORLEY

The Other War

I.
Uncertain whether we'll expire
lolling in a bucket seat,
single-file on a path, or upright
in a briefing room

as walls roll back like curtains
furling on a smoking stage, we undertake
each duty in a brother's place,
ill-equipped to sort civilians from those actors
trying merely to survive.

II.
Causeless in their wire coils,
surveyors push devices into lines
strung below a plank where feet will fall
decisive as a trigger pull before
the earth erupts.

III.
The sleepless know the soul's jihad, fought within
or out as times demand, accounting death
as murder or just consequence,
solid only to the bones
we mend, break, love.

Foreign Policies

Natural cycles brook no defeat; as rolling
boulders of snow manhandle all comers in a path
toward earth's lowest point, so too does violated
nature resound in expanding rings of consequence
and change. The miracle of a moment surrenders to decay
in the twinkling of a solar ray, and the proudest
monuments of man go down to earth
unwarrantied. Or so goes the joke in Afghanistan,

that place intemperate sons vowed to bomb
back to a stone age from which it was not far
removed. My time there began when cooler heads
binned strategies of revenge and planned
in fury's aftermath to light the flame of liberty
inside Afghan homes. In Kabul, a city bounded in a basin
made by the Hindu Kush, there is one secure block,
and inside that block an international base.
On that base, a Croatian cafe and an office building
built by Soviets share an alley. The Americans go
in through an armored door, turn right to the stairs, and descend
to the basement E.C.P. where clearance is confirmed. Those who know
why they are there don't always get through. Those who pass
surrender cards for a badge, leave cell phones on a
rack, and enter a humming warren of stone walls lined
with the minimum number of air conditioning units necessary
to defeat the combined furnace of C.P.U.s and human meat.

The cave goes deep, and cheap A/Cs follow laws
of gravity and vapor. A plastic tube dangles from each one
into a bucket emptied twice a day. Twenty-four hours
of freedom-loving breath converts to eight gallons of water waste.

LIAM CORLEY

On most days, I join analysts to convey brimming pails
up stairs to the alley and derisively declare, "Gardyloo,"
as the condensed secrets of our days spill onto a muddy path.

We tramp back with dirt caked on our boots,
a cargo deposited hundreds of times per day on the stairs
and floors of liberty's anti-Bin Laden cave. The dust congeals
fine ash descending from air, the native earth, and our sloughing
skins. We police this threat to machines and bronchial health
several times a week with brooms and placebo vacuums
that move the dust from floor to air with a businesslike whine
that sounds as if it happens in a home. The cinders come from smashed
apartment complexes and surrounding shell-scarred shacks
where the Kabuli poor burn long-collected feces to stay warm
through bitter nights they've known all their lives. Their shit rises
in a meagre stream through the winter sky until it cools, drifts into
our classified domain, and lodges in soft tissues that function
as baleen between the passage of a mouth and the lungs within.

No more than once per day we bear another
burden up the stairs: a clear plastic bag of the finest
crosscut shred, powdered remains of knowledge
we've gained and have chosen to destroy. More profligate
than the surrounding poor, we incinerate our dust.
The Slovakian fire brigade superintends flames
that convert our work to ash that rises on tenebrous wings
above the portals of the blasted city's unrelenting lungs.

Care Package

Boxes from known names came stuffed
with flavors to hoard, use as currency,
devour as a second childhood.
After rifling through ones marked "any sailor,
airman, soldier, or Marine" for coffee bags
and better razors, we send
hard candy, deodorant, and all
the other bric-a-brac
to Chaps as aid for the Kabuli poor
who may yet outlive
our being here.

From one I draw a knitted cap and breathe
stale air, wool yarn, and the musk
of a Mankato granny suffering painful joints
for the sake of our shaved and coverless heads.

That night a 6-year-old froze,
stretched out by her brother and mom;
a klick away I dozed in fatigues
beside a green terry robe on a hook.

This I want America
to see: a gap-toothed child
sucking on a watermelon
Jolly Rancher, a taste foreign
as the clacking of needles in a warm
midwestern home. Why,

she asks.
I don't know. I guess it's just
a way to support
the troops.

LIAM CORLEY

CIVCAS Nine-Line
(The U.S. Army uses a 9-question medical-evacuation request format to maintain clear and organized communications)

LINE 1:   *Location of pick-up site*

                on the road
                in the middle of the way
                between enlistments
                in front of Mustafa's house
                page-two news
                where Yuri bought it in eighty-three
                her uncle's fenderless sedan

LINE 2:   *Radio frequency and call sign*

                sign-language con brio
                5.56 and .50-cal
                200-foot command wire
                spirit-rapping
                wails

LINE 3:   *Number of patients by medical precedence*

                the specialist is urgent and so is the 12-year-old,
                already buried in the blue burqa of her first blood
                POTUS seeks priority for a second term
                the rest are all routine

LINE 4:   *Special equipment required*

                a precise sense of vulnerability
                a plan
                historical perspective
                a hoist capable of lifting six dumb-struck passengers
                      out of a self-fulfilling prophecy
                tomorrow

LINE 5:   *Number of patients by ability to move*

                two litters
                five ambulatory
                thirty-two million by word of mouth

LINE 6:   *Security at pick-up site*

                engaged at nine and three
                no safer on base or at home
                feuding families allied in a fight

LINE 7:   *Method of marking pick-up site*

                a single puff of white smoke
                14-pica point
                a fresh hulk by the side of the road
                the shrill keening of prayer

LINE 8:   *Patient nationality and status*

                us
                them
                the open-bordered state of the dead

LIAM CORLEY

LINE 9: *Terrain and site contamination*

    deserts lapping at snow-covered peaks
    ground water shot with dissipating blood
    half-life of one endlessly repeating blast

Transcript from the Night News

Her news cannot be found
on the World Wide Web, women's health worker
on the back of a husband's motorcycle,
kicking up dust in Farah City. He escorts
her to the job, as a man must do, in a secure
part of town where adolescents exchange
cell phone videos of a slow beheading.
                              Barricades
will shift to catch the latest threat, no telling
where they'll appear or if the danger
lies in stopping there. So as the
husband slows and wonders if he should take
another road, he doesn't think the grip
that tightens on his side more than love
preparing for a change. What she sees
she sees through eyes accustomed
to the signs of medical distress
in furtive wives swathed
head-to-toe in protective dress. The easy
task would be to strafe them passing by.
Instead, they pull her from the seat
soldered to the cycle's back when the clinic
opened for her work, pan her husband's head
so that he takes it in, and throw her to the ground.
Serially they kick her face and shoot her
vaginally. Behind them, the lad with greatest
resolution gets the hit on video. They leave
the husband trembling at her side
to be passed from relatives' hand to hand
with a simple script inscribed
inside his eyes, why am I left alive?

Something Else You Don't Need

Nudged awake by a loud enough
report, I pull near
the armor, helmet, and gun I know
the Big Mike will call for soon.

The Macedonians at the gate
survive, swaddled in checkpoints
manned by Afghan police, their history
not yet repeated.

Just Tuesday I walked past their HESCO barrier
and ducked around a concrete wall. Unaccountable,
the chicle boy I didn't buy from last week
holds out his hand again,
in it a pack of something
I don't need. Today he tumbled upward
like a leaf blown back to an awestruck
branch, tossed like my girl as she flies confiding
from my arms.

Only Tuesday he plucked a pen from my sleeve,
bold like so many urchins I've met in marketplaces or on
roadsides free of an overseeing eye.

Knowing how this type of news spreads,
I put the dime-store pen in a pocket, saving it
for some form to fill out, some check
in a box,

where it lies still in a bin,
buried between the drop-down

UNWOUND

holster and boots that never fit
right, no good even
for this, the story of its life.

LIAM CORLEY

Pathfinder and Chingachgook in Colloquy (Leatherstocking Poem No. 2)

This poem depicts James Fenimore Cooper's protagonist, Nathaniel "Natty" Bumppo, during an evening watch. He stands with his lifelong companion, Chingachgook, whose name translates to English from the Delaware language as "The Great Serpent."

I serve the white man's god and thank him for his gifts,
for trails that left the settlements and brought an orphaned boy
to fires of the Delaware. I don't expect I'll see your Manitou after death,
Chingachgook, when our scalps or hearts are torn away.
I've heard the white man's god has made a white man's heaven,
and I think myself no better than the fate allotted to my kind. Ahh,
but you sing, Great Serpent, of a happy hunting ground
where your father waits upon the trail to stalk a buck
wise Uncas saved in spring for winter meals. It pains my heart,
old friend, to think you'll creep along that path
    and my Killdeer keep peace.

What I've been taught of a white man's life after death
would not tempt a Mohican's pride: rest, peace, and no pains
to make a body know it's quickened back to life. I can't make out
the justice that would part two warriors no Mingoes
ever could defeat while one stood to keep the other free.
Many a common meal has made us one blood, sagamore,
but not wiser than our people's gifts. I am a white man
though my heart is Delaware; I won't turn from paths
my people call good, just as I take no scalps in war.
On your belt, dried skin and hair make the ladies sing loud,
and every ear around the council fire opens wide

UNWOUND

to let your words go in. Though I make no torture or my own revenge,
I've been happy in your triumphs of that sort.

How the matter ends we'll leave in this pipe, a gift of yours
we've taken. Light it as the fires burn low, and let
its pale smoke sear the ancient breath we share.

Mentioned in Dispatches

BLUF (Bottom-Line Up-Front)

"Crossing the river
brings a great empire
down." Admire the Pythia as we will,
even plain truth and calibrated
probability cannot prevent besotted consumers
from a wayward path.

"What king, when he sets out to war,
will not first sit down
and consider?" So says
the Prince of Peace, ever
an economist of blood.

Cast the bones,
dry bones,
and tell me, son of man,
what the dead say
about the harvest
of a future fight.

No shame, prophet,
to hide your face
inside your face
that you may see
the better hand taken
by the shitty one
you dealt.

LIAM CORLEY

Intelligence Report

SPOTREP: tonight
the living sons harvest
poppy stalks, dry and sweet,
and burn the scant fields clean.

A mined road
extending from the village heart
leads to men smoking
in the hulk of a Soviet A.P.C,
nodding as the conversation turns
to the next zakat,
who will pay
and how.

Fingering another spot
on the map, an elder cracks
pistachios. Shells pile up
on shura mats; each one speaks
to the unhelmeted commander whose hams
ache as he squats in the circle and weeks
after when he reports
to the scene of an unexploded I.E.D.

One smiling face has valleys deeper than
the Korengal, lines marked by
years of squinting against the sun
and an enemy's silhouette.

Last to leave, he moves from pine
to pine, disappearing in the shade
of trees whose roots split rocks
and anchor in this hardened place.

Negotiations

In the governor's office, the provincial
police chief, the city police chief, and the secret
police chief disagree about whose men
have failed to stop the bombs. They all use
English, but only the governor has studied
abroad. He speaks of Buffalo between each pitch,
deftly shelling a tray of nuts.
"If I had more men ..."   "If my men
were better paid ..."   "If
we had more guns ..."
They smile. Then the situation might improve.

The talk centers on one chief
they declare a threat. A cell blares for incoming,
and they pause. The governor smiles and takes it.
Pashto streams from his lips; his whole body speaks.
The chiefs resume their harangue beneath
his guffaws. A misunderstanding,
when the call completes. The bombs
were just a mistake. He thought I
wanted him arrested, that I had another
for his post. The governor offers me
pistachios. There will be no more bombs.
I told him he has my entire
trust. He presses his hands away as though
refusing a gift: No more bombs. The secret
chief begins again. "A library ... how can such a place
be kept safe? Better to spend
on men who make us strong today."

The pistachios come from Badghis. *Bad guys*

LIAM CORLEY

in Badghis, we joke when safely back on base.
Our 'terp won't say what was in the governor's call.
To hear what's private is impolite. And then,
Besides, I was listening to you. I smile.
Of course. You have my entire
trust. The 'terp moves to the door. "See you tomorrow."
      "Yes. Tomorrow." His cell
rings. "I have to take this."
bringing the receiver to his ear. "I know," and I go back
to where the day began.

Heavy Guns at Alexander's Citadel

Dismounted on a tourist trip,
we walk in armor along
the softly crenellated lip
surrounding Shar-e-Farahdun.

A secure perimeter offers
independence, so our line
splays out along the berms
of two millennia, if we grant
the interpreter's boast.

Staff Sergeant Wilkie smirks
first: "Seems like Alexander
built every town, fucked
every malik's daughter to put
some other shithole on the map."

Heavy guns rumble in the east;
their near report pulls taut
the gravity between us.

Specialist Sharpe, on point,
finds the provincial governor's guards
firing into a mute wall, .50-cal.
chewing away what time had crusted there.

Upon comms, we stand down, relieved to be
just in company with another flock of vandals.

Loosening a Kevlar strap, I bum a smoke
from Daoud and make him laugh by
lighting it off their *DISH-Kuh's* barrel, just like
Marines in Inchon used to do.

LIAM CORLEY

Uncleared

Carrie Prejean's breasts
plaster walls in place
of pred' porn too classified
to grace the eyes of local
electricians wiring the joint
to glow, nor of their supervisor,
Ahmad, who owns the firm
and likes to watch his men
do U.S. contract work.

All but holy eyes
follow Carrie's strut
through nightly news, lips
wet in the righteous
proclamation of
a reigning queen. Sucking
air through gaps in teeth,
the holy look instead at guns
adorning foreign hips and stacked on—
what a rack!—armor-bearers
men call trees. Such was the shop

that General Nofun
Infidel fixed when he forbad
a *fraa-jee-lay* fishnet leg lamp
marketed by the Old Spaghetti
Factory as a welcome sign of home
and holidays even in July.

Carrying the Bags

They use mirrors under trucks,
fashioned like inverted detectors
the metal-hunters use on beaches
to find lost change. Here the stakes go up
as undercarriage views may reveal
the signs of bulky, makeshift bombs—a care-
less wire or recent weld. More outlandishly,
a man or two might hang
concealed in wheel wells
like stowaways on flights to
Heathrow found mangled and inert
upon arrival. Two men at least
conduct the checks: one to watch
the glass and the other to observe
the driver's eyes as he endures.
This truck is full of dirty laundry
said to be returning cleaned
by Daoud and Nabil, cousins contracted
to wash the clothes of servicemen
fifty-three countries have sent
to soil themselves in Afghanistan.

Tonga and Malaysia, Iceland and Ukraine—
these are countries that must pay
to have their clothes
soaked and spun dry, stains
and dirt combining to a uniform
greyish green. Nothing white
remains: underwear
and socks take on the shades
of starry nights spent in bunkers

LIAM CORLEY

staring at a distant minaret
with an enviable line of sight
behind the compound walls.

Daoud's the more social one,
gleaning tricks of daily greetings
along with slang
that make him sound more like
a New York cabbie than a Nuristani
boy. Nabil depends
upon a Cheshire smile, nodding away
the patter clients pay
to one who serves.

A mirror fastened to their wall
at the spot where waiting ends
seems a vain addition to the
serviceable decor. Men
delivering bags pause
before it as their eyes verify
the washed-out faces it displays
remain their sullied own.

Why the Cop Let Me Go

First thing he asks after "Do you know how fast
you were going?" is, "Military tags? You in the Navy?"
Anyone who knows, knows I am
by a decal beneath the windshield sticker. That's why
I sit straight when civilians make a scene, avoid argument
for its own sake, and make no statements
indicating anger or regret.

Turns out his brother is deployed. Navy. Kabul.
A few questions later, I figure where he's at: "I was
there last summer. Not a tidy place when
the south wind blows." The south wind always blows, like it blows
today on the eastern side of the Sierra Nevadas, lifting
the dried-out bed of Mono Lake and sending it to rest
in eyes that squint along a Mojave Desert road
not far from where the Afghan scenes of Iron Man
were shot. Stalling, I inquire, "How often do you write?"

More talk. He wonders what his brother needs,
what hazards on his roads are like. I sugar-
coat it some. No point in making him upset. "The base
is only bad when suicides assault. Then everyone's
on lock-down for a month. Armor all the time. No loitering
on breaks. Send him good smokes, something he can trade
with A.N.A. for a taste of homemade aush and na'an." He grunts
and walks through dust to his idling car.

My wife is boiling at my side. "Oh, my God, you're getting off,"
she says as he comes back, my license
in his hand. "I can't believe you're getting off."

LIAM CORLEY

Now he tells me going slow will keep me safe,
gives me back my paperwork,
sends me on my way.

"He'll be OK," I reply. "He'll come back safe.
Just like me." After the cop pulls out, I sit and breathe
some long seconds, eyes in line with streaks
undulating on the tarmac road ahead,
wife saying something I don't understand
about what a lucky bastard I am.

In Which I Serve as Outside Reader on General Petraeus's Dissertation

The U.S. Army's/Marine Corps' Field Manual on Counterinsurgency, FM 3-24 (2006), has origins in a 1987 doctoral dissertation on Vietnam, written by the manual's co-author, then-Army Lt. Gen. David Petraeus

Premise flows from premise like water over the edge
of a waterfall, entrancing those not caught
in the turbid spray, those not lingering in the limestone
chutes that channel the first descent. *Dulce et decorum*,
those molecules in free fall, powerless to reverse
dictates of gravity, whether they be composed
of dollars or bodies. A theorist must maintain sense of scale,
must view war at an appropriate distance, so that its beauty
may emerge like a cold, perfect moon that draws the restless
from their beds with dreams of space flight. The best way to lie
is to get one big whopper on the table and move on quick
to crystalline truth after truth in a train of plausibility
so compelling we don't see how down becomes
up, so convinced are we by the quality of our reasoning
that be leads to see and eventually to eff and tee, and the best
first lie aligns with ones we've already bought, like how we cheer
Frost's traveler in the yellow woods longing for the road
not taken, nodding along with his glib boast that non-
conformity explains contingency because we can accept
failures chosen on noble grounds more than unforeseen
leaf-covered ways that erupt when footfalls complete
the circuit of pressure-plate I.E.D.s. Mr. Petraeus,
    your counterinsurgency
tools could only work in countries we didn't create,
    republics not birthed
by death from above, and so I regretfully conclude
this dissertation presents the naked assertion of imperial power
as the contribution of a helpful guest, final proof that
intelligence and gulled innocence, in general, betray us.

LIAM CORLEY

La Longue Carabine Grieves (Leatherstocking Poem No. 3)

This poem depicts James Fenimore Cooper's protagonist, Nathaniel "Natty" Bumppo, upon witnessing the death of Uncas, who is the son of Chingachgook and the eponymous "Last of the Mohicans."

Uncas, *Le Cerf Agile*, you surge ahead too boldly,
yet not so boldly as your courage and your love. You are noble,
but exposed. Pull back a little until I give Magua,
Le Reynard Subtil, a kiss from Killdeer's lips and free
that girl who draws you too soon from the sapling cover
other warriors thread their way through. Fall back,
I say. That fox will stumble before mid-day. I would have felled
him by now but fear for his fair captive stays my hand
and blinds my hate. I wish him dead but cannot fire.

So many bodies I love in peril yet I cannot speak
    with Killdeer's tongue—
Oh God, make Uncas as patient as me! Justice never looks green,
yet it ripens to a sweetness that sags the bough into our grasp.
Oh God, why should Uncas die?

The shot that fells my brother's son—
the shot
my brother
my son—
the shot.

My tardy finger pulls and takes the breath from the turncoat fox.
I hammer with God's hand and know only God's remorse
for lovers dead and their defiler an unrepentant corpse.

UNWOUND

Already you sing, Chingachgook. Your son dead. His enemy dead.
His flowering love dead. The grandchildren unborn,
    that unconceived tribe
of red, and black, and white, who might have buried
    our bones and carried on
our fight.

Ah me, the rifle brings no end to pain. Only songs
may rise, and I with one note,
one syllable of grief,
do sing.

Thank You for Sending Me

Dedication

For the female exec whose new nanny half-said
that she hoped she would put her own daughter to bed;
for the second-tour sergeant still planning patrols
around known ambush sites and freshly dug holes;

for the teacher appraising the work left undone
by a class more impressed with the cost of a gun;
for all laboring people who've learned how to fight
for a piece of their mind from the unthinking night,

I offer a few of my tricks of the trade
useful in binding decisions I've made.
Tell yourself that disasters aren't always your fault;
given time, the complaining will gradually halt.

Do the work that's required to survive every day
without quenching the spirits you find on the way.

LIAM CORLEY

Call Me Ahab

The professor dips a scholar's pen
into the fount of soldier's sore;
the plume he wields now traffics in
taxonomies of gore.

An unexpected charge along the path
gives the soldier sole possession of the bottom line.
Now the professor takes a round,
engraves it with a message for the afterlife.

The soldier locks
the bearer in his sights,
surrenders speaking
of his rights,
and makes the academic
voice a groan
of inarticulated stone.

The body drops.
Buried with its mate,
the mind is meet
and, swelling the emblazoned hide,
fuels microbic heat.

Thank You for Sending Me

I want to ask each thankful one who's quietly appalled
by the effluvia and mud through which their servant crawled:
do you drive? Does your wallet burst with unacknowledged effects
of the military-industrial-entertainment complex?
I can't for the life of me explain where in history to begin.
Kosovo? Somalia? Gateway drugs for humanitarian
wars cosmopolitans claim we must resolutely wage
or sink ourselves and global wealth into a new dark age.
The true quagmire lies in American thought: unable
to legislate a partisan détente, we claim the mantle
of opposing problems we can't ourselves beat back
by sending drones to scapegoat states more open to attack.
Intellectual pride has more K.I.A.s than religious hate;
all who merely vote succor enemies of the state.

LIAM CORLEY

One War

> *"The art of losing isn't hard to master [...]"*
> —Elizabeth Bishop, *"One Art"*

Your Congress wants to hear about the war.
Complete this form. In order to compare,
you must count the way they did before.

Every game needs stiffs to keep the score,
and you're the joe they tagged for ours. Don't swear
when Congress wants to hear about the war.

Scrubbing firefights is now your chore.
Bury ones where we shot first or you'll scare
the aides who count the way they did before.

Listing casualties by month makes more
of them than using weeks, and that's not fair
when Congress wants to hear about the war.

Green-on-Blue is new, so just ignore
those dead when they don't fall in columns where
you're told to count the way they did before.

D.C. won't see what their money's gone for
without this form to show 'em that you care.
Your Congress wants to hear about the war,
but you? You count like those who've gone before.

Reserves

Frank had grown accustomed
to rebellious teens. Joe thought he knew
the ways to minimize a loss. Oscar was impressed
by well-maintained machines. Dan said he didn't mind
not acting like the boss.

Alice joined us
to get off the beaten track. Kenzo fell behind the times
his kids would tweet. Jackson wasn't someone
who you thought would crack. Adam joked about the weirdos
on his beat.

Bonnie was never easy
unless behind the wheel. Twyla saw through lies
like any mother would. Will talked about his sleep
more than our last meal. Shad could graph the cycles
of congealing blood.

All fought to hold their peace about the war except
in consequential dreams encrypted while they slept.

LIAM CORLEY

Not Now that Strength

Yellow trucks the color of sand trickle down a defile,
staggered by good doctrine on the intervals of a mile.
The convoy rallies at a point just beyond the village
where scouts survey their six and twelve all along a ridge.
No blast disrupts the flow of bodies and machines. What failed
to happen to us then left holes no decoration quelled.

Corky has the gut we said he would when he falls in
behind Thoreau who's filling out another dumb petition.
Kendall pressed his B.D.U.s into haut couture;
Marisol stamps her muddy boots till there's no manure.
I see Allen slip off a tie before he answers up.
The Major sounds off loud, and then he spits into a cup.
Shannon says she hasn't missed the eyes she always sensed;
I remain the one who pees whenever chance presents.

Two ghosts appear to be unchanged: Perez, who killed himself
on checking in at Bliss, and Jones, who lasted long enough
to drive the truck he bought at Arifjan. Though Walsh can't wait
to get back out on point, cautious children infiltrate
our perimeter with bottles full of substances
we no more suspect. We let them mob their armored aunts,
uncles, moms, and dads who duck behind the yellow doors
for hurried hugs and news before they turn them back to chores.

Like Ulysses's unnamed crew in Alfred's honored lie,
we know that kings and heroes all return alone or die.
Uneasy on the printed sheets, we toss beneath our shield
and grind the gears of yellow trucks until we yield, we yield.

Dirt Navy

Anchor's away, my friends,
the light ship has cast its bonds
and risen on the cloud of dust
the rotors press upon.

The green weeds we see sway
are climbing up the walls
of seabags stacked on crosshatch flats
and winched tilled 'master calls.

O captain, my captain has fallen low
in grade; his petty officers still salute,
their crow's an eagle made.

Bearing new clothes
and guns, small bores and column rights,
our khaki mess is all undone, and signal
lamps are lights. Cold

comfort then this ribbon that
marks our own small war, a becalmed
army left to drift on you,
our foreign shore.

LIAM CORLEY

Recessional
for Andrew

A man receding toward the sun
becomes the beast he rides upon;
the silhouetted, shrinking man
descends into Afghanistan.

Darkness pools from West to East
when the airborne torch retreats,
and what is seen in western skies
now casts a shadow in our eyes.

The text displayed by dying day
shows the way a corpse can pray
in colors bloomed before the clot
turned red to black and black to naught

but hell fire from its Maker's hands
that burns night more than light demands.

Father Jacob Gets His Limp

A limb of the soul, broken and refused, aches
when barometric pressures on the heart
recall a moral wounding that mistakes
a loss inflicted for a willing part.

Irradiating thought, the pain escapes
in waves of guilt or innocence dismayed
from shrapnel lodged within synaptic tapes
that wake the dead whenever they are played.

How unforeseen the pang that splits our core
when gaming boys respectfully request
to know how many we have killed in war:
the one confirmed remains inside this chest.

Returning as a patriarch at night,
alone, in pain, a concentrated debt
of foreign ghosts, of haloed fear, we fight
the brawny angel of a just regret.

What would we give to grieve them less? The truth?
Or conscience pricked to life by brokenness?
Wrapping arms around protesting youth,
we blow the joint the angel turned to bless.

LIAM CORLEY

Natty in the Stocks
(Leatherstocking Poem No. 4)

*This poem follows James Fenimore Cooper's protagonist,
Nathaniel "Natty" Bumppo, after he has been convicted for killing a deer
out of season.*

Judge, I did my part in the business of '76
as a scout and so maintained my independence
without a soldier's pay, though many a Mingo
and King's man were by my muzzle felled.
I gave counsel face-to-face to generals
and their like and never was gainsaid
but to my hearers' harm. Listen to me now.

These stocks keep my grey head low, and men who would fear
to meet me in the woods fill my ears with hard words. Boys
who were not born when I had seen near sixty winters pelt me
with hog's feed. I paid your fine for the buck I killed
though my gizzard burns to confess as wrong
a deed that but a year ago would have been my right.
Many a hungry mouth has taken venison from my hand
at no cost or even call for thanks. The Lord's bounty
is for all, and no law can take His gifts away.

Ah me, the bite of these planks on my neck and wrists
makes me think hard thoughts of you, Judge.
When the panther met your child in a place your court will never tame,
she rejoiced my eyes did not water as they seem to now, for by them
    I made a mighty shot
that saved her from the creature's claw. You say that's not material
since I did willfully obstruct a sheriff and your warrant to invade
a hut that sheltered naught but an old man's thoughts and days.
I can't think much of a law that has such scoundrels to enforce it.

That I should live to see such times, ah me! But lass,
this hour will not be my end. With Master Pump
at my left in these stocks and you standing like a queen upon my right,
I'll bear a morning's watch penned as a forest beast. My curses
give way to peace. There now, no tears.
Give the mockers no delight. Let them feast on naught but spite.

Nothing / Happening

Terminal Leave

The unarmored
shoes she dons
leave space in the toe
for a soul. A phantom
hanging on her thigh
slips past
the mind's
control.

Circles she's in
wheel slowly.
She cracks jokes that go over
like lead.
The flag once borne
on a shoulder
now fatigues a frame
by her bed.

Eyes that once
were beside
watch her recede
into night; pills
the V.A. prescribed
count down
like rounds.
in a fight.

LIAM CORLEY

In Case of Emergency, Break This Poem

A poem curls bright fumes across a packed room,
making all the quitters rub their lips and smolder.
Young poems fart in an elevator. Lead tailings of night
poems pinwheel in a watershed. Old poems fire words
in a crowd.

This poem is a woman on the Metro shouting through her phone.
Don't stare. She's not talking
to you. Is this even your train? Lake Street only moves
those who don't mind the tang of urine from upstream.

I keep poems at home, bags stacked in the garage. What I do
in my own house is none of your damn
business. The H.O.A. sends a letter. My poems stink.
You'll see, I mutter. Auden was right: poetry
makes nothing happen.

When that shit blows up,
people ask, What was that? Oh, that's
nothing, I say. Nothing's
happening.

O.P.M. Hacker Blues

In 2013 and 2014, Chinese government hackers compromised servers at the U.S. Office of Personnel Management and exfiltrated the personnel and security records of several million American service members.

Wei Lin Da strains over the river of his target's
life: mother-in-law, friends, high school jobs,
first apartment after college, two sisters
living in different states. Wei's terminal butts against
five others, hexagonal one-upmanship.

Wei wonders if his target's house is too small
for three kids and a new wife, 1,424 square feet
not quite meeting the American standard. In Beijing,
Wei, 34 and well-employed, lives with his parents
and meets his girlfriend for weekend trysts.
If he flips this case, he'll climb up
apartment lists. Scrolling through asset-tracking data,
Wei finds the mortgage has never been late;
under water in 2010, Zillow hints
the house now floats on a modest bubble of equity.

Wei digs for another in. How to parse
password: *R@bb!tRedux0329*
Numbers cross-reference to anniversary
with ex-wife. *Where's she?* Two cities away.
Wei puts the date in a tumbler and trawls for more.

His eyes burn, no telling if from cigarettes,
Beijing air, or hours spent unblinking
at a screen. Wei's sore back tells him he needs
a vacation, like this one in Aruba

LIAM CORLEY

the ex has booked for next month. If only
his man headed there he'd have him.
What's his Expedia name? Wei's cell

phone rings in a box with forty others,
stashed in the lobby of a Deep Panda
front. The message, when retrieved,
will speak of another dinner missed
at the stand-up noodle shop six blocks

down. Gnawing on a bitter peel, Wei stares
at yesterday's post of a smiling man whose carefree arms
rest on children he only has in partial custody.

Wei spits into a bowl and winces at the time.
Doesn't he know we own him?

Double Rainbow at Dawn, 15 North at the 10

The rubberneckers slow down
as they do for other hazards,
brake lights merging into
the penumbra of a double rainbow
due west of the traffic lanes,
while in the East the rising sun
irradiates vapor-soaked air.

We are all late, looking askance
at the fireworks of nature,
wondering how our priorities
match up with this display.

Double, not just one: two arcs
of vibrant color proclaiming
peace on earth if we
don't kill each other
trying to take it in.

LIAM CORLEY

November 11 in Southern California

City trucks finally respond to the uphill neighbors' house
after a two-day gusher has flushed
the common gutter clean. Standing in their driveway,
the downhill neighbors scream
about things past due.

Between these homes she shelters.
Packed inside the garage, a laminate
pocket guide murmurs
hostile acts, and the empty
bladder of a CamelBak sighs.

In the back, giggling children
like the fingers of a hand
run in and out of trampolines and tree houses,
making believe they are victors
where her mind is.

Passing small bills from a change tray
to a bum when she stops by his light,
she prays the "God bless" that he gives her
pays down her homecoming's price.

If You Give a Vet a Pencil

If you give a vet a pencil,
she'll ask you for a spring-assisted knife to sharpen it.
When you bring the drop-point tanto,
she'll ask you for some lubricant.
When you bring the liquid silicone,
she'll ask you for free Wi-Fi.
When you register her device,
she'll post a picture of her carbon scrawl and get flamed
by other vets who claim
no one ever gave them a pencil.

LIAM CORLEY

A Veteran Considers the Republic and Remembers Ginsberg

America, I've given you all, and now I'm less than one percent.

America, fourteen-point-six-seven-five years of service I can't
     characterize as other-than-honorable,
three-hundred-ninety-one days pounding dirt
     in other people's countries,
and one-hundred-seventeen sleepless nights per annum in perpetuity,
September 11, 2017.

America, I'm willing to renegotiate our social contract. I won't
     complain about the clean bill of health
charged against me by the V.A., and you can stop involuntarily
     mobilizing memes of my demise
in support of indecent campaigns. America, believe me when I say
I'm not dead broke, I ain't so straight, I'm not all white,
     and I don't love hate.

America, when will you realize we are peopled with two-and-a-half
     times more African-Americans than veterans,
discounting three million souls in both tribes? Here I incorporate
     them all,
the ones hunted and penned in an inglorious spot, survivors whose lives
     matter,
because we both know the wary grief of looking at a uniform we paid
     for and wondering
whom the man beneath has sworn to protect and defend.

America, into this veteran poem I will take all the graduates of
     Columbine and Sandy Hook,

UNWOUND

the ones who lived after having no answers for the warm muzzle of a
    gun, and their teachers,
especially the ones who ran toward shots. The hall
    of the American Legion
will overflow with such heroes, streaming like the blessed dead
    of Fort Hood and Chattanooga
across the Styx in Charon's commandeered craft,
    the open door of welcome
forced, as always, by warriors still living.

America, let's rent a cherry picker to take down the F
    in the V.F.W. sign,
let what is removed drop horribly in the pail. Police will gather
    in their surplus riot gear
and nod in understanding fashion, their years of service trailing them
    like a sentence,
arming them with arcane questions of whether civilians we protected
    yesterday will kill us today.
America, out of the sands of Kandahar and Ramadi, I go with them too.

Furthermore, America, in this election season, I go with righteous
    immigrants and refugees,
fellow sufferers of long journeys in inhumane transports that leave
    them in permanent pain.
O, my desperate ones, border-crossers of unwilling countries, you who
    pay taxes of sweat and fear,
you are not alien to me, or my thirty-five thousand brother and sister
    dreamers in green and khaki
fighting for something that isn't wholly ours in dangerous places
    where we simply do our jobs.

America, when will you give Cyber Purple Hearts to all who have had
    their lives taken out of your senile, digital grip,
starting with the twenty-four million whose secrets you've let slip into

LIAM CORLEY

    China's voracious panda pocket?
We shall update and tweet ourselves feverish with the chant,
    "Uncle Sam is my Big Brother"
in protest of all those Xis and Putins and Snowdens and Kims
and Transnational Criminal Elements stealing our binary essence.
I'm not joking, America: I foresee the day when every iPhone
    will be issued with a trauma kit,
every laptop with a liability release for unauthorized remote access.

O America, my love, my burial plot, all this I will put
    in a phantom poem,
my own republic, for you to receive, a sea bag of sights unseen
to tumble down the ramp of a decommissioned C-130,
this empty box,
this absent limb.

Leatherstocking in the Furnace (Leatherstocking Poem No. 5)

This poem follows James Fenimore Cooper's protagonist, Nathaniel "Natty" Bumppo, when he and his party have been trapped by a wildfire intentionally set by their enemies.

I am a used-up old man, a miserable trapper whose own hide
will last but a few winters more. If dying is our task today,
I can do it with no loss. The clever devils lit the prairie,
and that's a steed we can't outrun. Dumb beasts
already drum the earth, but soon the fiery flood
will drown them in their smoky flight. Stop, lad, and think,
or the flower slip of girl beside you will kindle in an awful way.
The black smoke billows over yon swelling ridge. But a moment more
and swift flames will break its line and rise like sudden dawn.

Hold, hold! You cannot charge so. Ah me, that courage
    should be traitor
to a little sense. You would die brave, as youngsters often do,
but your striving would be vain. The inferno we face
won't be breasted in a bound. Patience serves us more
than the best mare in this Lenape's herd. We must not run.

If you would live, hear now a trapper who has long hunted these plains:
quickly cut the tallest grass and mound it as a bulwark here.
    Then dig graves
in open earth; cut the turf in strips and let red clods paint your flesh.
No, lass, I give no counsel of despair. Snug in these weedy beds,
the furnace will o'errun us. We cannot fight such times, boy,
yet we will outlast defeat.
                  Here bursts the roaring storm.
The thrumming gusts overwhelm our ears like Niagara's endless falls,

LIAM CORLEY

and heat beats upon my cheek through a wide palm's
shield of sward. All air pounds from my chest, and I am limp
as beaten meal in a baker's bag.

Ha! The maelstrom lessens even at its height.
The fire leaps like an arrow loosed from a warrior's full-drawn bow,
and flames you might have fed scatter faster than a lightning bolt.

Now will I rise and cackle like a laying hen. Though all around
lie smoking clumps, we'll wash our faces in Missouri's flow by dusk.
Ah me, children in each other's arms, you are a joyous sight. I thank
the Lord above you did not take flight.

Frame of Reference

I tell my friend I am writing a science-fiction novel. Oh, like "Star Wars"? I love that movie. No, I reply, I am writing a novel. It has a double plot. A man's world is ending, and so is his marriage.

I liked that in "Interstellar," she says. Does your planet explode? Are there blasters? You need guns for special effects. My pages don't boom, I admit. No flashing lights. Just words.

People like that? What about a soundtrack? That worked for "Guardians." Your book should have a soundtrack. Why not put out a playlist, tell people which chapter gets which song?

I shake my head sorrowfully. No music either. Too much happens in a vacuum. You need air for vibration. It's not fair, she says. No one has trouble breathing in the movies. What about

the science? Are drives warped? Can you beam anywhere? I'm embarrassed. My science is fine. No one travels. They can't figure out why things don't work. Their best people

get blown up. That's good, she says. Blown-up is good. The bigger the better, I agree. And the cat? How does it get saved? Ahh. The cats. Yes, I have them. They eat people.

Her eyebrow lifts. I don't think it works that way. What about your hero? Who plays him on screen? You'll need star power. I think about that. The man is kind of average. Me, I guess.

You are not attractive, she says. That's true, I say. That's why I'm writing a science-fiction novel. A man's world is ending. It always is, she says. You need a better plot. I do, I say. I do.

LIAM CORLEY

At the Children's Hospital

On one wall, faces in remission glow
next to mosaic notes and crayoned
praise. An unused light-box
on the other wall lies at forehead
height to make for easy viewing.
Seated at the desk between, the oncologist
studies pixels on a screen. He thinks
he knows where this is going, pulls
another shot, and steels himself
for the shock that always follows.
He stands and kneads his skull,
drops his head against the box.
Coughing first, the nurse sees nothing,
asks if Mrs. Gee can come in now.
The doctor nods and lifts his eyes
from the growing dark inside. Her boy
is sleeping in the room beside, exhausted
by the nerves she shields him from.
He knows why she wouldn't let the studio
photographer comb his hair away.
His hand is tangled in it now, cradling a lobe,
and when he wakes he'll see the sun
setting over Anaheim, raise his hand
against its rays and see the bones as dark
as locks of hair upon his mother's palm.

Hagar at Nine

Sitting long at table
with a daughter who refuses
the meal mother made,
I think of your thin wrists
skin-deep with the blue
veins of aspiration.

This maiden's world revolves without words.
Its sun goes continually down
to promising stars smearing night
with no answers
for our impetuous
questions.

My daughter's lonely eyes
fill with the hurt yours
always concealed.

After mother's words
release, she is as quick to scramble
onto a counter-
top for a bowl
to hold her store-
bought grain as you were to take
the bottle and the loaf.

She is hungry, was hungry
all the time, for more
than hunter's meat,
more than angels' signs.

LIAM CORLEY

Open Letter

She presses warm into my side against the winter wind,
chattering about her day and how she did not know I was me.
Twice she walked past open doors and saw but did not see
the man I am, medaled and stiff in dress blues,
waiting for her eleventh birthday song. I watched her flit
    behind the doors
to giggle with her friends and wonder who the soldier waits for
    at their school.
The nation's cloth makes me strange; even the teacher can't perceive.
She texts my wife, "I didn't know until I saw them leave."

The only thing my father sought in his dead mother's house
was a letter opener fashioned like a Mameluke sword,
his gift to her upon his feared commission. The replica was perfect
in my boyhood eyes, with hanging braid and scabbard
    I longed to flourish
in prepubescent play. After school and home
alone, I'd scour the house for trouble, rifle through his closet
for the love of hefting hidden guns. At twelve, I found, beneath the bed
    where he
and mother lay, the full-sized blade, his thirteen-year companion
and now my favorite toy.

To his grief, the tiny Mameluke never came to light, and I want to
    mount
the real one on a wall so I'll be sure to find it when he's gone.
The noblest gifts are those we long to keep
no matter how far back the wound when they were given.

The Task in Which We Walk Together

I know why my 9-year-
old daughter likes horses, guinea pigs,
and rescue-shelter dogs. Animals
are patient. They do not demand
intention be put into words or that she
choose between expression and defeat.
They let her body speak and listen
to her eyes say please.

This is why I hold her in
my arms before I urge
her to the gate that separates
humanity from beasts. Give her

her head go gentle on
the reins she knows where the
clover lies and will step between
the rocks if you'll let her talk
to her with knees and small
leans whisper in her ears if you must
no words but love

Notes & Acknowledgements

Further background regarding my series of "Leatherstocking Poems," which are embedded in various parts of this collection:

> *The Leatherstocking Tales* (1823-1841) are a series of novels by James Fenimore Cooper (1789-1851). They tell the story of one of the most beloved characters in American fiction, Nathaniel "Natty" Bumppo, a white frontiersman raised and educated in Native American societies. The character is variously known as "the Leatherstocking," "the Deerslayer," "*La Longue Carabine*," "Hawkeye," and "the Pathfinder." Alongside Bumppo, the Mohegan warrior Chingachgook emerges as a central figure in the saga's elegiac portrayal of American origins.

❖ ❖ ❖

I am grateful to the editors of the following magazines and journals, in which these poems first appeared—some in slightly different versions:

"**At the Children's Hospital**" first appeared in *The Hippocrates Prize*, Hippocrates Press, 2013. It received a second-place Hippocrates Prize for Poetry and Medicine.

"**BLUF**" first appeared in *Inlandia: A Literary Journey*, Volume 9, Winter 2019

"**Care Package**" first appeared in *Proud to Be: Writing by American Warriors, Vol. 1*, Southeast Missouri State University Press, 2012

"**Double Rainbow at Dawn, 15 North at the 10**" first appeared in *The Wrath-Bearing Tree*, April 2019

"**Father Jacob Gets His Limp**" first appeared in *Proud to Be: Writing by American Warriors, Vol. 3*, Southeast Missouri State University Press, 2014

"**Frame of Reference**" first appeared in *Strange Horizons*, Nov. 1, 2021

"**Improvised Explosive Device**" first appeared in *The Line Literary Review*, Spring 2021

LIAM CORLEY

"**In-Country**" first appeared in *Inlandia: A Literary Journey*, Vol. 9, Winter 2019

"**Intelligence Report**" first appeared in *Proud to Be: Writing by American Warriors, Vol. 3*, Southeast Missouri State University Press, 2014

"**In Which I Serve as Outside Reader on General Petraeus's Dissertation**" first appeared in *The Wrath-Bearing Tree*, April 2019

"**One War**" first appeared in *The Line Literary Review*, Spring 2021

"**Something Else You Don't Need**" first appeared in *Proud to Be: Writing by American Warriors, Vol. 1*, Southeast Missouri State University Press, 2012

"**Terminal Leave**" first appeared in *First Things* No. 248, December 2014

"**A Veteran Observes the Republic and Remembers Ginsberg**" first appeared in *The Wrath-Bearing Tree*, March 2018

"**Why the Cop Let Me Go**" first appeared in *War, Literature, & the Arts Journal*, Vol. 31, 2019

"**Unwound**" first appeared in *Chautauqua* No. 9, 2012. It was a finalist in the 2011 Chautauqua Institute Poetry Contest

Glossary

A/C: Air-Conditioning

A.N.A.: Afghan National Army

A.P.C.: "Armored Personnel Carrier"

Arifjan: A city in Kuwait. Camp Arifjan is a nearby U.S. military installation that is used as a forward logistics base.

B.D.U.: "Battle Dress Uniform." A U.S. camouflage uniform worn in combat.

"Big Mike" (a.k.a. "Big Voice"): Slang term for a public-address system often found on larger Forward Operating Bases ("FOB").

Bit: In American slang, "two-bit" means inferior, cheap, worthless, or insignificant; "worth approximately 25-cents." In nautical terms, a "bitt" (two "T") is pair of posts on the deck of a ship for fastening mooring lines or cables.

BLUF ("Bluff"): "Bottom-Line Up-Front." A military writing technique that emphasizes stating purpose and conclusions prior to supporting analysis.

CamelBak: A trademarked brand of personal hydration system, often consisting of a water-bladder worn on the back.

"Chaps": Generic, non-personal nickname for a military chaplain.

CIVCAS ("Sihv-Kaz"): An incident involving civilian casualties—people killed or injured.

C.P.U.: "Central Processing Unit"; a computer microprocessor

Dragon Skin: A trademarked brand of personal body armor. In the mid-2000s, some U.S. troops acquired Dragon Skin products because they were rumored to be more effective than government-issued equipment.

Dog-tag: A metal disc or badge, embossed with personal identification data, worn by military personnel around the neck or laced into the boot.

DShK ("DISH-Kuh"): A Soviet heavy machine-gun similar to the U.S. M2 Browning. Often mounted on a tripod or wheeled carriage.

E.C.P.: Entry Control Point

5.56 ("Five-Point-Five-Six" or "Five-Five-Six"): The 5.56-by-45mm rifle round is the standard bullet cartridge used by NATO-member militaries.

.50-cal. ("fifty-kal"): A .50-caliber bullet cartridge is one-half-inch in diameter. In the U.S. military, the term ".50-cal" can refer to the type of ammunition, or to the M2 Browning heavy machine gun that uses it.

Green-on-Blue: In U.S. military map systems, blue-colored symbols identify friendly (U.S.) units, while green-colored symbols identify friendly (allied; host-nation) units. "Green-on-Blue" describes incidents in which members of friendly forces commit violence (example: assassinations) against U.S. troops.

HESCO ("HESS-koh"): A manufacturer of modular bag-and-cage barrier systems, which, when filled with sand or other material, can be used to protect military facilities.

H.O.A.: Homeowners' Association

Humvee: High-Mobility Multipurpose Wheeled Vehicle (HMMWV). A family of 4-wheeled military utility trucks.

I.B.A.: Individual Body Armor

Kevlar: A synthetic fiber of high tensile strength used in the construction of protective gear such as military helmets and vests.

Le Cerf Agile: "The bounding elk" (French)

Le Reynard Subtil: "The subtle fox" (French)

Mameluke sword: A slightly curved, scimitar-like sword traditionally worn by U.S. Marine Corps officers in dress uniform.

MOLLE ("Molly"): MOdular Lightweight Load-carrying Equipment. A system of military backpacks and other items, onto which pouches, tools, and other add-ons may be attached using standardized fasteners.

M.F.A.: "Master of Fine Arts." A graduate degree, often in writing.

POTUS ("POH-tuss"): President Of The United States

Seabee: Nickname for U.S. Navy Construction Battalion ("C.B.") personnel.

SERE ("SERE"): Survival, Evasion, Resistance, and Escape training. The word "sere" also means "dry or without moisture."

Shura: In Muslim traditions, a form of public consultation. Can be similar to an organizational town hall or council meeting, in which many parties voice opinions toward an informed decision.

SPOTREP ("SPOT-rehp"): "Spot Report"

T.A.Y.H.: "The Army You Have." During a December 2014 public Q&A session while visiting with U.S. troops in Kuwait, U.S. Secretary of Defense Donald A. Rumsfeld responded to a question from U.S. Army Spc. Thomas "Jerry" Wilson. Wilson had asked about why he and his fellow soldiers were scrounging for scrap metal in order to increase their unarmored wheeled vehicles' resistance to bullets and shrapnel. A widely reported version of Rumsfeld's response was interpreted by many as brusque: "You go to war with the army you have, not the army you might want or wish to have at a later time."

'Terp: Slang for "Interpreter." Often a civilian contractor of varying fluencies in English and host-nation languages, who may wear U.S. military uniform but not rank.

V.F.W.: Veterans of Foreign Wars of the United States. A Veterans Service Organization (V.S.O.) founded after the Spanish-American War. Members must have deployed to any foreign conflict for which a campaign or expeditionary medal has been issued.

Zakat: In Muslim traditions, a form of almsgiving. One of the five Quranic obligations of Islam.

LIAM CORLEY

A Few Words of Thanks

The composition of poems always involves community, imagined or actual. Most of these poems were inspired by people and events I encountered overseas, but those memories came into literary form because of my urge to connect with fellow citizens, academics, and family members at home who had borne my absences and deserved some insight into what they meant, at least to me.

Aaron DeRosa was a generous and shrewd reader of many early drafts. His encouragement and collaboration in hosting the Cal Poly Poets Circle made the joy of creation fiercer through sharing the flame with others. I'm grateful also to all of the students who created with us in the Poets Circle.

Don Kraemer, Alison Baker, John Edlund, Liliane Fucaloro, Sharon Hilles, Olga Griswold, and Edward Rocklin encouraged my creative work and supported me in the difficult chrysalis of bringing a military voice into my academic home.

The editors of *Chautauqua*, *First Things*, and *The Wrath-Bearing Tree* helped me reach my first readers, for which my gratitude endures.

Hilary Lithgow, Peter Molin, Will Ruger, Roger Thompson, Alexis Hart, Mariana Grohowski, Jim Dubinsky, Randy Brown, Tracy Crow, Andria Williams, Amalie Flynn, Paula Weston Solano, Elke Azpeitia, and Donald Anderson have all tended the humus of veteran writing from which creativity sprouts. May your tribe increase!

Ryan Winters, Steve Zelt, Chris Davidson, Marc Malandra, Paul Lake, Farzana Marie, Tim Courtney, Sheila Rodriguez, and Ashley Wu are all fellow travelers whose voices and example have been significant at different stages of the journey.

I am tremendously grateful to Jehanne Dubrow, celebrated author of nine books of poetry, including two books I particularly admire, *Dots & Dashes* and *Stateside,* for her kind words on my work.

Many thanks also to my fellow sailors Jillian Danback-McGhan (author of the short-fiction collection *Midwatch*), novelist Travis Klempan (*Have Snakes, Need Birds*), and Benjamin B. White *(Always Ready: Poems from a Life in the U.S. Coast Guard).* Your encouraging words helped me through the final stretch of publication.

Finally, my family has been subject, audience, and inspiration for much of my art. Thank you, Amy, for listening to my poems hot from the forge, even though poetry isn't your cup of tea, and to Stephen, Clare, Dorothy, and Sam for bearing with my outbursts of verse at the dining room table.

Author's Statement

I turned to poetry after my first deployment because I had no patience for simple answers—the lies we tell others and ourselves to avoid too close an examination of our complicity in the atrocity of any war, just or not. I was angry, guilty, and accusatory, but I was also dispositionally opposed to laying the burden of those feelings on colleagues, strangers, and family members whose questions—some casual, some earnest—triggered them.

However, I also didn't want to become the caricature of a veteran muttering in the corner, "You just had to be there." Instead, I hope that transporting readers—"taking them there," psychologically and emotionally—can be accomplished through the medium of poetry, and that the results might lead to common understanding.

I was also painfully aware, as Ralph Waldo Emerson asserts in "The American Scholar," that I did not possess even half of my deployment experiences until I had distilled them into words, something I had no opportunity to do until years after events left their marks. I am, in every essential way, the first audience for these poems, as I've squeezed and refined them from the wounds of inarticulate experience.

I remain deeply convinced that homefront and battlefront are intimately entwined in modern wars, especially when waged by democratic 21st century societies, whose emotional and political lives are regulated through high- and low-brow art to degrees unprecedented in human history. Thus, I have availed myself of every medium to make evident our common wounding, common guilt, for the violence we've sustained and inflicted over the past twenty years.

Memoir, science fiction, and in this volume, poetry—I am driven to write in hopes that beauty and meaning emerge from the chrysalis of words woven from our dark violence. Redemption is too powerful a claim for what these words pursue. Tribute, then.

—Liam Corley

About the Author

Liam Corley is a professor of American Literature at California State Polytechnic University, Pomona. His work on literature and war has been published in *War, Literature, & the Arts, College English*, the *Journal of Veterans Studies*, and the *Chronicle of Higher Education*. His current academic project, *The Voice of the Veteran in Eighteenth and Nineteenth-Century American Literature*, has received a year-long research fellowship from the National Endowment for the Humanities (NEH).

Corley is the author of *Determined Dreamer: Bayard Taylor and America's Rise* (Bucknell University Press, 2014). A debut science-fiction novel, *Changelings: Insurgence*, is forthcoming from MilSpeak Books.

Liam is an award-winning poet whose work most commonly explores military experience and contradictions within American society. His poetry has appeared in *First Things, Chautauqua, The Wrath-Bearing Tree, Strange Horizons, O-Dark-Thirty, Inlandia, Badlands*, and *War, Literature, & the Arts*, the latter a journal published on the campus of the U.S. Air Force Academy. His poems have also appeared in multiple volumes of the anthology series *Proud to Be: Writing by American Warriors*, published by Southeast Missouri State University Press.

Since 2004, Corley has served as an intelligence officer in the U.S. Navy Reserve. He has completed multiple deployments, including ones to Afghanistan and Iraq, and throughout the Pacific area of operations. He lives in southern California with his wife and four children.

Also from Middle West Press

anthology

Our Best War Stories:
Prize-winning Poetry & Prose
from the Col. Darron L. Wright Memorial Awards
Edited by Christopher Lyke

❖   ❖   ❖

poetry collections

The Time War Takes
by Jessi M. Atherton

Hugging This Rock: Poems of Earth & Sky, Love & War
by Eric Chandler

Permanent Change of Station and *FORCES*
by Lisa Stice

Always Ready: Poems from a Life in the U.S. Coast Guard
by Benjamin B. White

September Eleventh: an epic poem, in fragments
by Amalie Flynn

HEAT + PRESSURE: Poems from War
by Ben Weakley

Welcome to FOB Haiku: War Poems from Inside the Wire
by Randy Brown, a.k.a. "Charlie Sherpa"

Made in United States
Troutdale, OR
11/02/2023